Roadkill abc

Adair McPherson

Print information available on the last page

Rev. date: 09/14/2018

To order additional copies of this book, contact:
Xlibris
1-888-795-4274
www.Xlibris.com
Orders@Xlibris.com

Roadkill abc

Adair McPherson

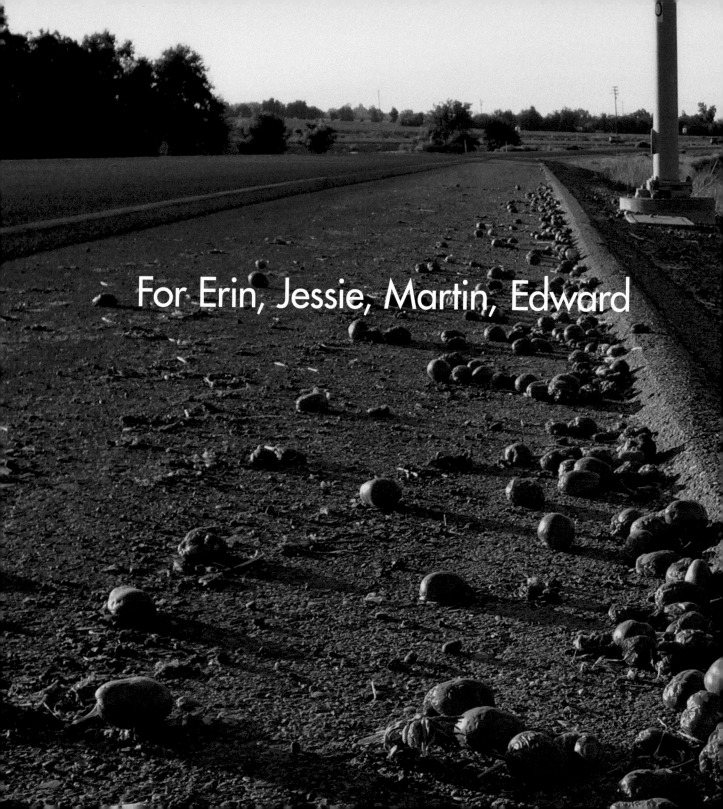

For Erin, Jessie, Martin, Edward

Thanks to Jake Miille for the photograph of the railroad crossing.

arm

b   **bear**

c   **candy**

d

dollar

e

earbuds

f

fly

g

glove

h   home

i insects

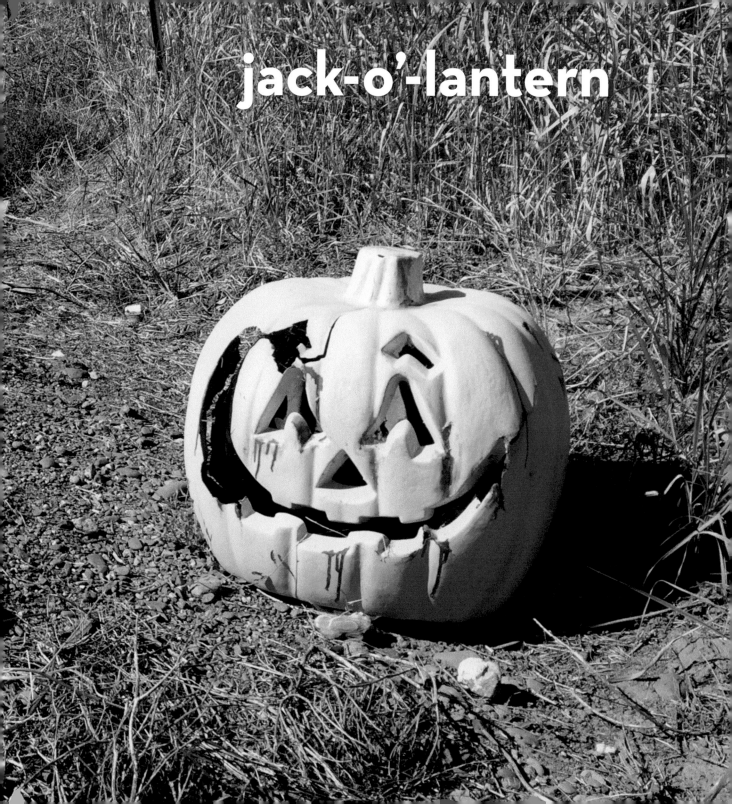

jack-o'-lantern

k

\kī-ˈō-tē\

l

lion

m   mattress

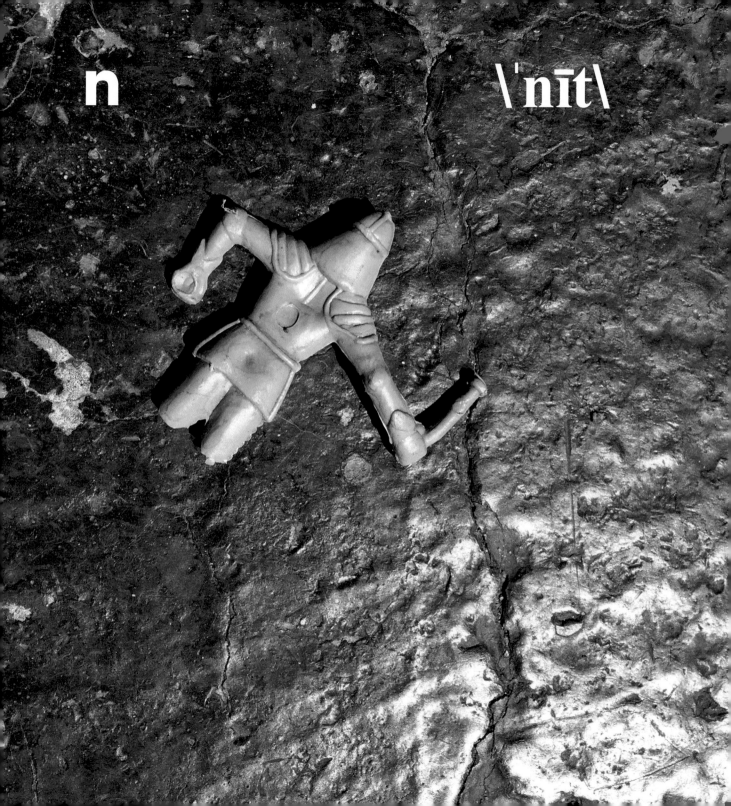

n

\\'nīt\\

owl

p

possum

q

quills

r

rat

s   snake

t

tree planter

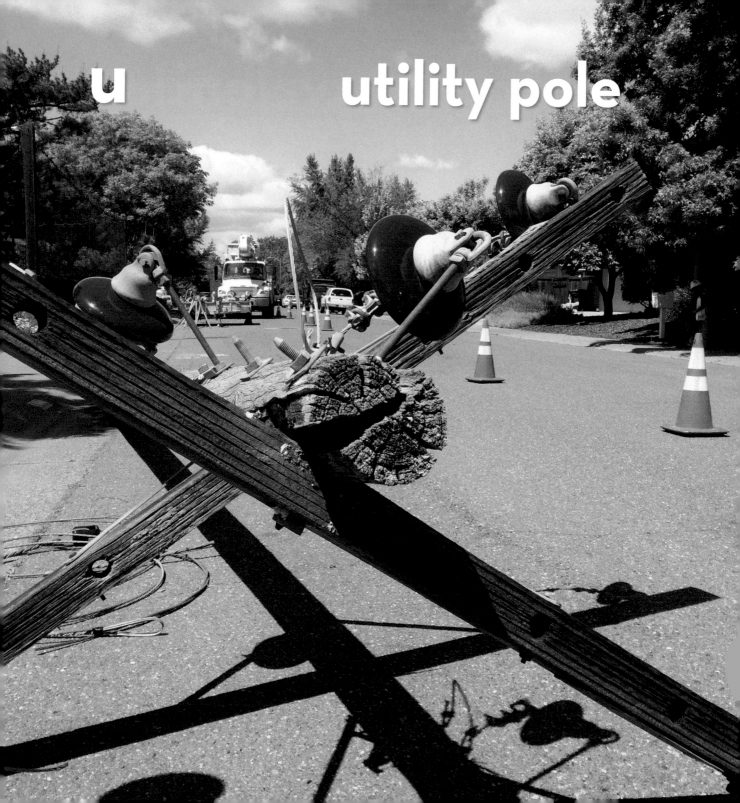

u   utility pole

v

valentine

w   watermelon

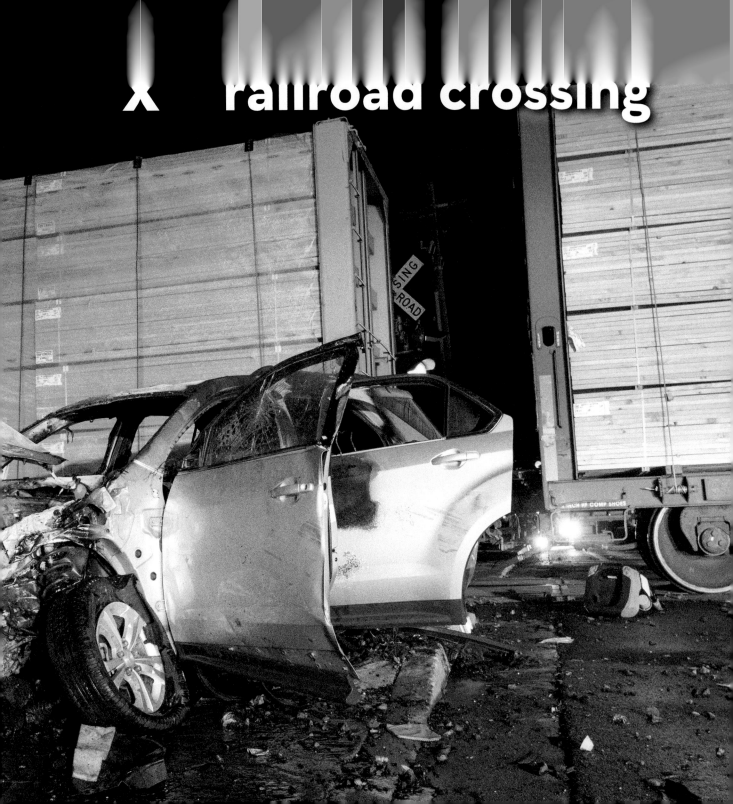

y

yucca

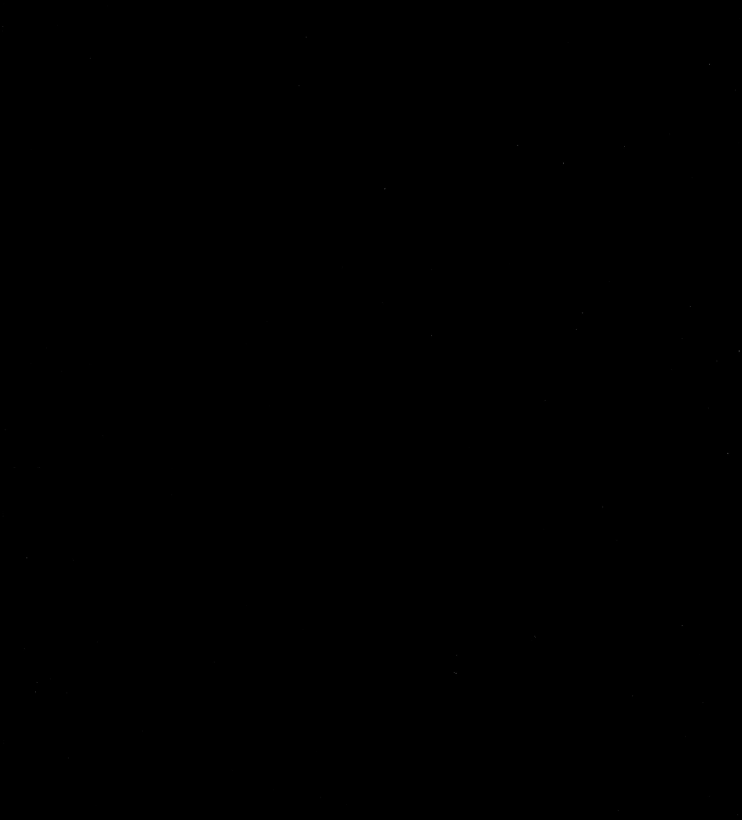

Printed in the United States
By Bookmasters